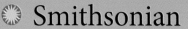

# Marie Curie

## The Woman Behind Radioactivity

Nancy Dickmann

raintree
a Capstone company — publishers for children

Raintree is an imprint of Capstone Global Library Limited, a company incorporated in England and Wales having its registered office at 264 Banbury Road, Oxford, OX2 7DY – Registered company number: 6695582

**www.raintree.co.uk**
myorders@raintree.co.uk

Editor: Jill Kalz
Designer: Kayla Rossow
Media researcher: Svetlana Zhurkin
Original illustrations © Capstone Global Library Limited 2020
Production Specialist: Tori Abraham
Originated by Capstone Global Library Ltd
Printed and bound in India

ISBN 978 1 4747 8677 5 (hardback)
ISBN 978 1 4747 8685 0 (paperback)

**British Library Cataloguing in Publication Data**
A full catalogue record for this book is available from the British Library.

**Acknowledgements**
We would like to thank the following for permission to use photographs: Alamy: Lebrecht Music & Arts, 7; Getty Image: Hulton Archive, cover; Library of Congress, 27; Mary Evans Picture Library, 23; Newscom: Album/Prisma, 13 (top), Everett Collection, 19, Heritage Images/Fine Art Images, 6, Heritage Images/The Print Collector, 13 (bottom), MAXPPP/IP3 Press/ Marlene Awaad, 29, World History Archive, 9 (top), 11, 17, 20, 25, 26; North Wind Picture Archives, 12; Shutterstock: Bjoern Wylezich, 14, Everett Historical, 5, 10, Humdan, 15 (bottom), Mark Kostich, 4, Morphart Creation, 9 (bottom), trabantos, 28; SuperStock: DeAgostini, 15 (top). Design Elements by Shutterstock

Our thanks to Emma Grahn, Spark!Lab Manager, Lemelson Center for the Study of Invention and Innovation, National Museum of American History, USA, for her invaluable help in the preparation of this book. We would also like to thank Kealy Gordon, Product Development Manager, and the following at Smithsonian Enterprises: Ellen Nanney, Licensing Manager; Brigid Ferraro, Vice President, Education and Consumer Products; and Carol LeBlanc, Senior Vice President, Education and Consumer Products.

# CONTENTS

Modern medicine is amazing! Doctors can heal bodies. They can treat diseases such as cancer. To treat diseases such as cancer they often use a treatment called radiation. It is based on a property called radioactivity.

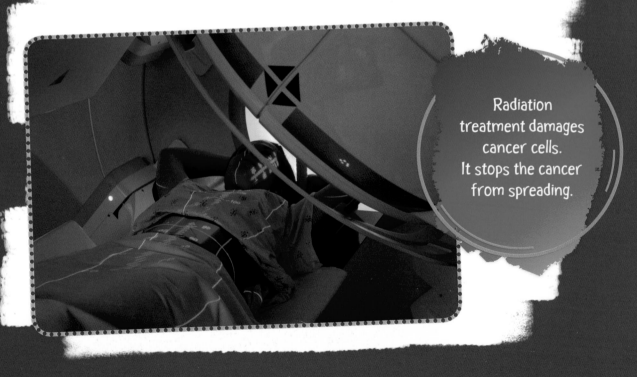

Radiation treatment damages cancer cells. It stops the cancer from spreading.

Why do we use radioactivity in medicine? It's all thanks to a scientist named Marie Curie! Scientists are people who study the natural world. They ask questions. They do experiments to find the answers.

Marie Curie was one of the world's most famous scientists.

# EARLY LIFE

Marie was born in Poland in 1867. Her parents were teachers, and they valued education. Marie loved learning. She worked hard at school. Her father taught her about science.

Marie's dream was to go to university. But back then in Poland, only boys were allowed. Marie didn't want to stop learning so she studied at a secret night school instead.

Marie at the age of 16

Marie's name at birth was Maria Sklodowska. She was the youngest of five children. Young Marie is seated in the middle in this photograph.

# SECRET SCHOOL

Poland's government controlled who could go to university. Some teachers started their own secret university. They taught anyone who wanted to learn. This was against the law. They met in secret at people's homes.

# STUDIES IN PARIS

Marie was very determined to learn. A university in France offered places to women to study there. Marie and her sister, Bronya, made a deal. They would help each other go to university there. They would take turns in working. First, Marie would find a job.

Marie paid for her sister to study in Paris. After her sister finished, it was Marie's turn to learn. The plan worked. In 1891 Marie moved to Paris. She studied physics, maths and chemistry.

Marie (left) with her sister, Bronya, in 1886

Marie went to university at the Sorbonne in Paris. Her sister had studied medicine there and became a doctor.

The courtyard of Sorbonne University

# PIERRE CURIE

Marie did well in her studies. She was given a project studying metals. But she needed a laboratory. A friend introduced her to Pierre Curie. He ran a chemistry lab. He let her work there.

Pierre and Marie Curie

Marie and Pierre fell in love. They were married in 1895. They worked together in the lab and became partners in life and in science. Marie wanted to be the first woman to earn a doctorate in science.

Pierre and Marie bought bikes for each other as wedding gifts. They rode their bikes around France on their honeymoon.

# RADIOACTIVITY

Radiation is energy travelling through space. Light is one form of radiation. There are other types of radiation too. In 1895, a new type, called X-rays, was discovered. X-rays could travel through solid objects.

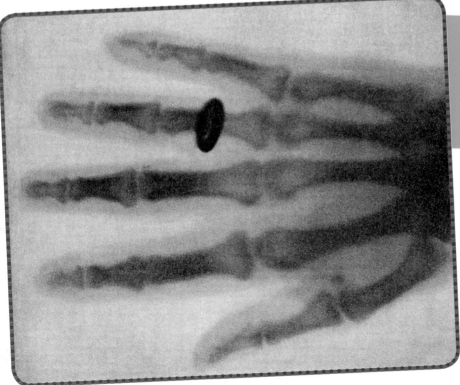

This X-ray photograph of a hand was taken in 1896 in Germany.

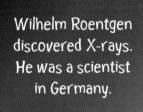

Wilhelm Roentgen discovered X-rays. He was a scientist in Germany.

Henri Becquerel

Then, scientist Henri Becquerel found that some materials give off radiation. Their atoms are unstable. They release tiny bits of matter. They also release energy. Marie Curie invented a word for this. She called it radioactivity.

# FINDING POLONIUM

Marie studied Becquerel rays. They came from uranium. She tested a mineral that contained uranium. But it gave off too much radiation. She guessed that it held another radioactive element.

The mineral Marie tested was called pitchblende.
Today it is known as uraninite.

Marie and Pierre at work in the lab

The Curies needed to find this other radioactive element. They used acid to break down the mineral. They removed some of its elements. What was left was very radioactive. The new element was in there. They called it polonium.

## Periodic Table of the Elements

# ELEMENTS

There are more than 100 different elements. Everything in the universe is made from them. Scientists keep looking for new elements.

# RADIUM

The Curies found another element. They called it radium. But it was a tiny amount. It was mixed with other things. No one could see or measure it. Some scientists did not believe their discovery.

Marie tried to separate the new elements. It took years of hard work. She used lots of pitchblende, which she ground and treated. At last she had a speck of nearly pure radium.

"I am among those who think that science has great beauty."
—Marie Curie

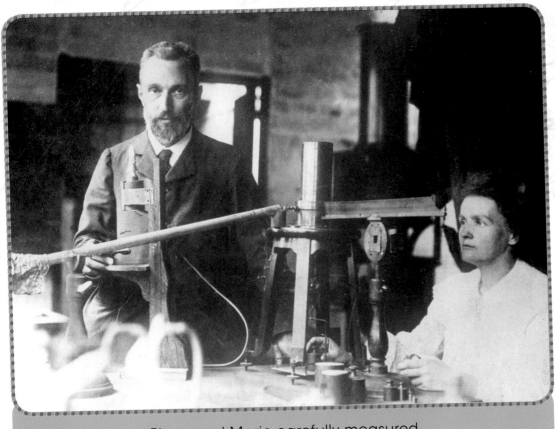

Pierre and Marie carefully measured
the radioactivity of new elements.

# ELEMENTS THE CURIES STUDIED

|  | Uranium | Polonium | Radium |
|---|---|---|---|
| Discovered | 1789 | 1898 | 1898 |
| Named after | Uranus | Poland | Latin for "ray" |
| Appearance | silvery | silvery-grey | soft, shiny, silvery |

# TRIUMPH AND TRAGEDY

In 1903 Marie and Pierre won the Nobel Prize in Physics for their work on radioactivity. The Nobel Prize is the world's top prize for this field of science. They shared the prize with Henri Becquerel.

Sadly, just three years later, Pierre died. He was killed in a road accident. He was only 46 years old. Marie had lost her husband. She had also lost her partner in the scientific research.

Nobel Prizes are awarded in physics, chemistry, medicine, literature and peace.

Pierre and Marie were a great team in scientific research.

# MAKING HER MARK

Pierre's death was shocking and sad. But Marie knew she had to go on. She became a professor and took over Pierre's job at the Sorbonne. Pierre's father helped to look after the Curies' daughters, Irène and Eve.

Marie continued her research after Pierre's death.

Marie finally separated pure radium. She won another Nobel Prize in 1911. This time she won on her own. The prize was for discovering radium and polonium. She was the first person to win twice.

Marie was the first female professor at the Sorbonne.

## WINNERS OF TWO NOBEL PRIZES

| NAME | FIRST PRIZE | SECOND PRIZE |
| --- | --- | --- |
| Marie Curie | 1903 (Physics) | 1911 (Chemistry) |
| Linus Pauling | 1954 (Chemistry) | 1962 (Peace) |
| John Bardeen | 1956 (Physics) | 1972 (Physics) |
| Frederick Sanger | 1958 (Chemistry) | 1980 (Chemistry) |

# USING RADIOACTIVITY

Marie didn't care about being rich or famous. She wanted to make new discoveries. She wanted her discoveries to help people. X-rays could help doctors. Radiation could be used to treat cancer.

Radiation can also be deadly. At first no one knew how dangerous it was. Even Marie did not always stay safe. Working with radioactive materials made her ill.

"I am one of those who think . . . that humanity will draw more good than evil from new discoveries."

—Marie Curie

Both Pierre and Marie had suffered from the effects of radiation. They were tired all the time. The skin on their hands was cracked and scarred.

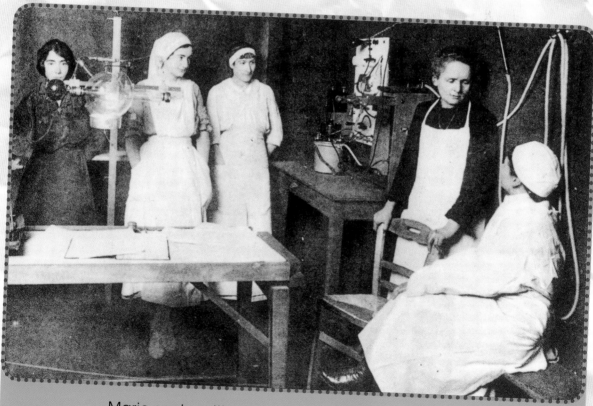

Marie spoke with nurses about radiation treatment.

# WORLD WAR I

In 1914 World War I began. Many soldiers were wounded. X-rays could help doctors find bullets. But there were few X-ray machines. They were in city hospitals, far away from the fighting.

Marie wanted to help. She helped by inventing a special car. It had an X-ray machine inside. She trained women to use the machines. Marie learned to drive. Now she could drive the mobile X-ray car to the battlefield.

Marie took X-ray machines to battlefields during World War I. People called the vehicles "petite Curies", or "little Curies".

## DOCTORS AT WAR

Army doctors had a hard job. They had to treat soldiers near the battlefield. They often worked in tents. They did not always have the best equipment. They were in danger from enemy attacks.

# MEDICAL RESEARCH

When the war was over, Marie went back to the lab. Her daughter Irène helped her. She was also a scientist. Marie started a new lab. It would help scientists find new ways to use radioactivity.

Irène Joliot-Curie won a Nobel Prize for chemistry in 1935.

Irène and Marie in 1925

Marie won many prizes. She gave speeches in other countries. She met many famous people, including scientist Albert Einstein. Marie died in 1934. Her work with radioactivity may have caused her illness.

Marie met two US presidents. She visited President Warren Harding (front) at the White House in Washington DC.

# CURIE'S LEGACY

We owe a lot to Marie Curie. She discovered two new elements. Her work helped us understand radioactivity. Now doctors can use it to help people.

Marie also broke down barriers for women. She worked hard to get an education. She showed that university was not just for boys. She proved that women could be scientists. Today there are brilliant female scientists all over the world!

A statue of Marie Curie stands in Warsaw, the capital city of Poland.

Today scientists at the Institut Curie in Paris continue Marie's work. They research new cancer treatments.

"Be less curious about people and more curious about ideas."

—Marie Curie

# GLOSSARY

**atom**  smallest particle of a substance that can exist

**cancer**  disease caused by abnormal cells growing out of control

**chemistry**  study of substances and their properties

**determined**  being sure about wanting to do something

**doctorate**  highest degree awarded by a university or college

**element**  natural substance that cannot be broken down into other substances

**laboratory**  room designed for scientific experiments, research or teaching

**matter**  anything that occupies space and has mass

**physics**  the study of matter and energy and their properties

**pitchblende**  mineral that contains uranium and radium

**radiation**  energy travelling through space

**radioactivity**  the giving off of radiation

**university**  place of study in which people gain degrees and carry out research

**uranium**  radioactive element

**X-ray**  form of energy that can pass through many materials

# COMPREHENSION QUESTIONS

1. The text on page 6 says that in Marie's time, women in Poland were not allowed to go to university. How is this different from education where you live today?

2. The text on page 10 describes how Marie met Pierre Curie. How did their meeting change her life?

3. How did Marie help soldiers during World War I?

# FIND OUT MORE

*Marie Curie* (Against the Odds), Claire Throp (Raintree, 2016)

*Marie Curie* (Super Scientists), Sarah Ridley (Franklin Watts, 2017)

*Who Was Marie Curie?* Megan Stine (Turtleback Books, 2014)

*Women in Science: 50 Fearless Pioneers Who Changed the World,* Rachel Ignotofsky (Wren & Rook, 2017)

# WEBSITES

*Marie Curie the Scientist*
mariecurie.org.uk/who/our-history/marie-curie-the-scientist

*The Genius of Marie Curie*
www.youtube.com/watch?v=w6JFRi0Qm_s

# INDEX